I0490633

Making Money on Youtube

Opportunities and Strategies for Success

By:

Asif Mahmood Anjum

Introduction of Book

In recent years, YouTube has emerged as one of the most powerful platforms for content creators and entrepreneurs to showcase their talents, skills, and knowledge while also making money. With over 2 billion monthly active users and an average watch time of 40 minutes per session, YouTube offers a vast audience that is hungry for high-quality, engaging, and informative content.

The rise of YouTube has also led to the emergence of a new generation of influencers and creators who are leveraging the platform to build their personal brands, connect with audiences, and generate income through a range of monetization strategies. From sponsored content and affiliate marketing to merchandise sales and crowdfunding, there are numerous ways for creators to turn their passion into a profitable career on YouTube.

However, achieving success on YouTube is not an easy task. With millions of videos uploaded every day, competition is fierce, and creators must be strategic, creative, and persistent in their approach. They need to develop a deep understanding of their target audience, create compelling content that resonates with viewers, and master the art of promotion and distribution to reach a wider audience.

In this guide, we will explore the various opportunities and strategies that creators can use to make money on YouTube. We will cover everything from the basics of setting up a YouTube channel and building a following to more advanced topics such as optimizing content for search and monetizing videos with ads and sponsorships. We will also share real-world examples and success stories from top YouTube creators who have built thriving businesses on the platform.

Whether you are an aspiring content creator or an established YouTube personality looking to take your channel to the next level, this guide will provide you with the insights, tools, and strategies you need to succeed on YouTube and turn your passion into a profitable career.

Index

There are many ways that content creators can monetize their YouTube channels and turn their passion into a profitable career. Here are 20 strategies and opportunities for making money on YouTube:

1. Advertising revenue: YouTube offers the opportunity to earn money through ads that run on your videos. The more views and engagement your videos receive, the more revenue you can earn.

2. Sponsorships: Brands may pay you to promote their products or services in your videos, usually in exchange for a fee or product samples.

3. Affiliate marketing: You can include affiliate links in your video descriptions, which generate revenue for you when viewers click on them and make a purchase.

4. Merchandise sales: You can sell merchandise related to your channel, such as t-shirts or mugs, to your fans.

5. Crowdfunding: You can use platforms like Patreon, Kickstarter, or Indiegogo to get financial support from your fans.

6. Super Chat: YouTube's Super Chat feature allows fans to pay to have their comments highlighted during live streams, providing creators with an additional revenue stream.

7. Channel memberships: YouTube also offers a feature where fans can become members of your channel, paying a monthly fee to access exclusive content and perks.

8. Fan funding: YouTube's Fan Funding feature allows viewers to donate money to support your channel.

9. Brand deals: You can work with brands to create sponsored content, such as a product review or demonstration.

10. Product placement: You can include branded products in your videos as a form of product placement.

11. Influencer marketing: You can work with brands as an influencer to promote their products to your audience.

12. YouTube Premium revenue: If your videos are part of YouTube Premium, you can earn a share of the revenue generated by the subscription service.

13. Content licensing: You can license your content to other websites, TV networks, or media companies, earning royalties for the use of your content.

14. Product reviews: You can earn money by reviewing products related to your channel niche.

15. Public speaking: If you have a large following, you may be invited to speak at events or conferences, earning a speaking fee.

16. Consultancy services: You can offer consultancy services related to your channel niche, such as social media marketing or branding.

17. Book deals: If you have established yourself as an expert in your niche, you may be able to secure a book deal to share your knowledge.

18. Brand partnerships: You can partner with brands on long-term campaigns or collaborations, earning a steady income over time.

19. Live events: You can organize live events, such as meet-and-greets or concerts, to connect with your fans and generate revenue.

20. Licensing music: If you create your own music for your videos, you can license it to other creators or media companies, earning royalties for its use.

(1)

Advertising revenue: YouTube offers the opportunity to earn money through ads that run on your videos. The more views and engagement your videos receive, the more revenue you can earn.

Advertising revenue is one of the most popular ways for content creators to monetize their YouTube channels. YouTube allows creators to earn a share of the revenue generated from ads that run on their videos. The more views and engagement a video receives, the more revenue a creator can earn.

The process of earning ad revenue on YouTube is straightforward. When you upload a video to your channel, YouTube will automatically place ads on your video. The ads can be in the form of display ads, overlay ads, or video ads. Advertisers pay to have their ads shown on YouTube, and YouTube shares a portion of that revenue with content creators.

To be eligible for ad revenue on YouTube, creators need to meet certain requirements. They must have at least 1,000 subscribers and 4,000 watch hours in the past 12 months. They also need to comply with YouTube's community guidelines and terms of service.

Once a creator meets these requirements, they can sign up for the YouTube Partner Program (YPP) and enable monetization on their channel. Creators can choose which videos they want to monetize and can also choose which types of ads they want to run on their videos. Creators can also choose the ad formats, such as skippable or non-skippable ads, that run on their videos.

The amount of money a creator earns from ad revenue on YouTube varies depending on a number of factors, such as the number of views, the engagement rate, the ad format, and the advertiser's budget. The revenue share for creators is typically around 55%, with the remaining 45% going to YouTube.

To maximize ad revenue on YouTube, creators need to create high-quality, engaging content that appeals to a wide audience. They also need to promote their videos on social media and other platforms to attract more viewers and increase engagement.

In addition to advertising revenue, creators can also earn money through other monetization strategies, such as sponsorships, merchandise sales, and affiliate marketing. By combining these strategies, creators can create multiple income streams and build a sustainable career on YouTube.

(2)

Sponsorships: Brands may pay you to promote their products or services in your videos, usually in exchange for a fee or product samples.

Sponsorships are a popular way for content creators to earn money on YouTube. Brands pay creators to promote their products or services in their videos, usually in exchange for a fee or product samples. Sponsorships can be a lucrative way for creators to monetize their channels, but it's important to approach them carefully to ensure they align with their values and content.

To land sponsorships on YouTube, creators need to build a strong brand and a loyal audience. Brands are looking for creators with engaged followers who are likely to be interested in their products or services. Creators should focus on creating high-quality content that appeals to their niche audience and use social media and other platforms to grow their following.

Once a creator has established a strong brand and following, they can start reaching out to brands or joining influencer marketing platforms to find sponsorships. Creators should look for brands that align with their values and content and negotiate a fair deal for their services. The fee for sponsorships can vary widely depending on the brand, the type of content, and the creator's audience size.

When creating sponsored content, it's important for creators to be transparent with their audience. YouTube requires creators to disclose sponsored content to their viewers, and creators should also make it clear when a video is sponsored in the title, description, or within the video itself. Creators should also be careful to create content that aligns with their values and their audience's interests. They should avoid promoting products or services that they don't believe in or that could harm their reputation.

To create effective sponsored content, creators should work closely with the brand to ensure the content meets their requirements while still fitting their channel's tone and style. Creators should also aim to create content that is engaging and valuable to their audience, rather than just promotional.

Sponsorships can be a great way for content creators to monetize their YouTube channels and build relationships with brands. However, creators need to approach them carefully and ensure they align with their values and content. By creating high-quality content and building a strong brand, creators can attract sponsorships that are both profitable and authentic.

(3)

Affiliate marketing: You can include affiliate links in your video descriptions, which generate revenue for you when viewers click on them and make a purchase.

Affiliate marketing is another popular way for content creators to monetize their YouTube channels. With affiliate marketing, creators can include affiliate links in their video descriptions, which generate revenue for them when viewers click on them and make a purchase. Affiliate marketing can be a great way to earn passive income on YouTube, but it requires careful selection of products and a strong understanding of your audience.

To get started with affiliate marketing on YouTube, creators need to join affiliate programs for products or services that are relevant to their channel's niche. Affiliate programs are typically run by retailers or other companies and provide creators with unique tracking links that they can include in their video descriptions. When a viewer clicks on the link and makes a purchase, the creator earns a commission on the sale.

To be successful with affiliate marketing on YouTube, creators need to carefully select the products or services they promote. They should choose products that are relevant to their niche and that their audience is likely

16

to be interested in. Creators should also disclose affiliate links in their video descriptions to be transparent with their viewers.

To maximize earnings from affiliate marketing, creators should focus on creating high-quality content that provides value to their audience. They should aim to create videos that educate, inform, or entertain their viewers and that feature products in a natural and authentic way. Creators can also use social media and other platforms to promote their affiliate links and reach a wider audience.

It's important for creators to be selective when choosing which affiliate programs to join. They should look for programs with fair commission rates and that provide high-quality products and services. Creators should also read the terms and conditions carefully and ensure that they comply with any guidelines or restrictions.

Affiliate marketing can be a lucrative way for content creators to earn passive income on YouTube. By carefully selecting products, creating high-quality content, and promoting their affiliate links, creators can generate revenue from their channels while providing value to their audience.

(4)

Merchandise sales: You can sell merchandise related to your channel, such as t-shirts or mugs, to your fans.

Merchandise **sales** can be a great way for content creators to monetize their YouTube channels while building their brand and engaging with their audience. Creators can sell merchandise related to their channel, such as t-shirts, hats, mugs, and other items, to their fans. By offering unique and high-quality merchandise, creators can build a loyal fan base and earn additional income from their channels.

To get started with merchandise sales on YouTube, creators need to design and create their products. They can work with a third-party company to handle the manufacturing and shipping of their products or do it themselves. Creators should focus on creating merchandise that reflects their brand and resonates with their audience. They can use their logo, catchphrases, or other unique elements from their channel to create merchandise that their fans will want to buy.

Once the merchandise is ready, creators can promote it on their channel, social media, and other platforms. They can create dedicated videos or posts showcasing their merchandise, and they can also offer special discounts or promotions to their fans. Creators should make it easy for their fans to purchase their merchandise by providing links in their video descriptions or social media posts.

To be successful with merchandise sales on YouTube, creators need to build a strong and loyal fan base. They should focus on creating high-quality content that engages and entertains their viewers and use social media and other platforms to build their following. Creators should also listen to their fans' feedback and use it to improve their products and offerings.

It's important for creators to ensure that their merchandise meets high-quality standards and is delivered to their fans in a timely manner. Creators should work with reputable companies or handle the manufacturing and shipping themselves to ensure that their fans receive high-quality products.

Merchandise sales can be a great way for content creators to monetize their YouTube channels while building their brand and engaging with their audience. By creating unique and high-quality products and promoting them effectively, creators can build a loyal fan base and earn additional income from their channels.

(5)

Crowdfunding: You can use platforms like Patreon, Kickstarter, or Indiegogo to get financial support from your fans.

Crowdfunding is another way for content creators to monetize their YouTube channels by getting financial support from their fans. There are several crowdfunding platforms available, such as Patreon, Kickstarter, and Indiegogo, that creators can use to raise funds to support their channel and create more content.

Patreon is a popular platform for content creators that allows them to receive monthly financial support from their fans. Creators can offer different membership tiers that provide exclusive content or benefits to their supporters, such as early access to videos, behind-the-scenes content, or personalized shoutouts. Patreon provides creators with a reliable source of income and allows them to focus on creating content without worrying about advertising revenue.

Kickstarter and Indiegogo are crowdfunding platforms that allow creators to launch projects and raise funds from their fans to bring their ideas to life. Creators can create a project page and set a fundraising goal, and their fans can pledge money to support the project. In return, creators can offer rewards to their backers, such as early access to the project or exclusive merchandise. Kickstarter and Indiegogo are great platforms for creators who want to launch a new product or create a special project that requires additional funding.

To be successful with crowdfunding on YouTube, creators need to have a strong and engaged fan base. They should focus on creating high-quality content that resonates with their audience and use social media and other platforms to build their following. Creators should also be transparent with their fans about their fundraising goals and how the money will be used.

It's important for creators to offer unique and valuable rewards to their supporters to encourage them to pledge their money. Rewards should be relevant to the creator's niche and should provide real value to their supporters. Creators should also set realistic fundraising goals and provide regular updates to their supporters to keep them engaged and informed about the progress of the project.

In summary, crowdfunding can be a great way for content creators to monetize their YouTube channels and receive financial support from their fans. By using platforms like Patreon, Kickstarter, or Indiegogo, creators can create unique and valuable content and products and build a loyal fan base that supports their channel.

(6)

Super Chat: YouTube's Super Chat feature allows fans to pay to have their comments highlighted during live streams, providing creators with an additional revenue stream.

Super Chat is a feature on YouTube that allows fans to pay to have their comments highlighted during live streams. When a fan sends a Super Chat message, their comment will appear in a different color and will be pinned to the top of the chat window for a certain period of time, depending on the amount they paid. Super Chat provides creators with an additional revenue stream and allows them to engage with their fans during live streams.

To use Super Chat, creators need to enable the feature on their YouTube channel and set up a payment account. Fans can then send Super Chat messages during live streams by clicking on the dollar sign in the chat window and selecting the amount they want to pay. Super Chat messages can be a great way for fans to support their favorite creators and have their comments seen by a larger audience.

Creators can use Super Chat to increase engagement during live streams and reward their most dedicated fans. They can provide special shoutouts or acknowledgments to fans who send Super Chat messages, which can encourage others to participate. Creators can also use Super Chat to provide exclusive content or rewards to their fans during live streams, such as early access to new videos or merchandise.

Super Chat is a simple and effective way for creators to monetize their live streams and build a stronger connection with their fans. However, creators should be mindful of their audience and ensure that they are not exploiting their fans for financial gain. They should also comply with YouTube's policies and guidelines regarding Super Chat usage, which prohibit certain types of content or behavior.

In summary, Super Chat is a feature on YouTube that allows fans to pay to have their comments highlighted during live streams, providing creators with an additional revenue stream. Creators can use Super Chat to increase engagement during live streams and reward their most dedicated fans. By using Super Chat in a responsible and ethical manner, creators can build a stronger connection with their fans and monetize their YouTube channels in a meaningful way.

(7)

Channel memberships: YouTube also offers a feature where fans can become members of your channel, paying a monthly fee to access exclusive content and perks.

Channel memberships is a feature on YouTube that allows fans to become members of a creator's channel by paying a monthly fee in exchange for exclusive content and perks. The feature is available to creators who meet certain eligibility criteria, such as having at least 30,000 subscribers and being part of the YouTube Partner Program.

Channel memberships provide creators with a reliable source of income and allow them to monetize their content beyond advertising revenue. By offering exclusive content and perks to their members, creators can build a stronger connection with their most dedicated fans and provide them with a unique and personalized experience.

To set up channel memberships, creators need to enable the feature on their YouTube channel and create membership tiers that provide different levels of access and benefits to their members. For example, creators can offer early access to videos, behind-the-scenes content, exclusive merchandise, or personalized shoutouts. Creators can also use channel memberships to create a sense of community among their fans, by offering access to private live streams or chat rooms.

Channel memberships are a great way for creators to build a sustainable business model on YouTube, by providing their fans with a value proposition that goes beyond free content. Memberships also provide creators with a predictable and recurring source of income, which allows them to invest more time and resources into creating high-quality content.

However, to be successful with channel memberships, creators need to have a strong and engaged fan base. They should focus on creating content that resonates with their audience and provides value to their members. Creators should also be transparent with their fans about the benefits of becoming a member and how their money will be used.

In summary, channel memberships is a feature on YouTube that allows fans to become members of a creator's channel by paying a monthly fee in exchange for exclusive content and perks. Channel memberships provide creators with a reliable source of income and allow them to monetize their content beyond advertising revenue. By using channel memberships in a responsible and ethical manner, creators can build a stronger connection with their fans and create a sustainable business model on YouTube.

(8)

Fan funding: YouTube's Fan Funding feature allows viewers to donate money to support your channel.

Fan Funding is a feature on YouTube that allows viewers to donate money to support their favorite creators. Viewers can make a one-time donation or set up a recurring monthly payment to provide ongoing support to the creator. The Fan Funding feature is available to creators who meet certain eligibility criteria, such as having a verified YouTube account and being in good standing with the YouTube community guidelines.

Fan Funding provides creators with an additional revenue stream and allows them to monetize their content beyond advertising revenue. Creators can use Fan Funding to fund new projects, improve the quality of their content, or cover production costs. The feature also provides creators with a way to engage with their most dedicated fan

s and reward them for their support.

To enable Fan Funding on their YouTube channel, creators need to set up a Google Wallet account and link it to their YouTube channel. Viewers can then donate money by clicking on the "Support" button on the creator's channel or video page. Creators can choose to display a message or personalized thank-you note to their supporters, which can increase engagement and encourage more donations.

Fan Funding is a simple and effective way for viewers to support their favorite creators and show their appreciation for the content they produce. It also provides creators with a way to connect with their fans on a deeper level and create a sense of community around their channel.

However, creators should be mindful of their audience and ensure that they are not exploiting their fans for financial gain. They should also comply with YouTube's policies and guidelines regarding Fan Funding usage, which prohibit certain types of content or behavior.

In summary, Fan Funding is a feature on YouTube that allows viewers to donate money to support their favorite creators. Fan Funding provides creators with an additional revenue stream and allows them to monetize their content beyond advertising revenue. By using Fan Funding in a responsible and ethical manner, creators can build a stronger connection with their fans and create a sustainable business model on YouTube.

(9)

Brand deals: You can work with brands to create sponsored content, such as a product review or demonstration.

Brand deals are a popular way for creators to earn money on YouTube by collaborating with brands to create sponsored content. A brand deal is essentially an agreement between a creator and a brand to produce content that promotes the brand's products or services in exchange for payment.

Working with brands to create sponsored content can be a lucrative way for creators to monetize their content, especially if they have a large and engaged audience. Brands are willing to pay creators to promote their products because it provides them with exposure to a wider audience and helps them to build brand awareness and loyalty.

To secure brand deals, creators need to have a strong and engaged audience that aligns with the brand's target market. Creators should also have a clear understanding of their brand values and ensure that the brands they work with align with their values and beliefs.

When creating sponsored content, it's important for creators to be transparent with their audience and clearly disclose that the content is sponsored. This helps to maintain the trust of their audience and ensures that they are not misleading their viewers in any way.

Creators can negotiate brand deals directly with brands, or they can work with third-party agencies or networks that connect them with brands. Third-party agencies and networks can provide creators with access to a wider range of brand deals and can help them to negotiate favorable terms.

When creating sponsored content, creators should focus on producing high-quality content that provides value to their audience and showcases the brand's products or services in an authentic and engaging way. By creating content that resonates with their audience and promotes the brand in a genuine and authentic way, creators can build a stronger connection with their audience and attract more brand deals in the future.

In summary, brand deals are a popular way for creators to monetize their content on YouTube by collaborating with brands to create sponsored content. By working with brands to promote their products or services in an authentic and engaging way, creators can earn money and build a stronger connection with their audience. However, it's important for creators to be transparent with their audience and ensure that they are promoting brands that align with their values and beliefs.

(10)

Product placement: You can include branded products in your videos as a form of product placement.

Product placement is another way for creators to monetize their content on YouTube by including branded products in their videos. Product placement involves featuring a product or brand within a video in a subtle and organic way, rather than explicitly promoting it.

When done correctly, product placement can be a highly effective way for brands to reach new audiences and for creators to earn money from their content. It can also be a great way for creators to add an extra layer of depth and authenticity to their videos, as they can incorporate real-life products and experiences into their content.

To effectively incorporate product placement into their content, creators need to ensure that the placement feels natural and authentic. This means that the product or brand should be seamlessly integrated into the video, rather than feeling forced or out of place.

Creators also need to ensure that they are disclosing any product placements to their audience in a clear and transparent way. The FTC requires creators to disclose any sponsored content, including product placements, to their audience to avoid misleading viewers.

One way to incorporate product placement into videos is by featuring products that align with the content of the video. For example, a fitness creator might feature a protein shake or workout gear in their video, while a food creator might feature a cooking tool or ingredient in their recipe.

Another way to incorporate product placement is by using branded products as props in a video. For example, a creator might use a branded laptop or smartphone in a video without explicitly promoting it, giving the audience a glimpse into the creator's real-life experiences and preferences.

Creators can negotiate product placement deals directly with brands or work with third-party agencies or networks that connect them with brands. As with brand deals, it's important for creators to ensure that the products they feature align with their values and beliefs and are relevant to their audience.

In summary, product placement is a way for creators to monetize their content on YouTube by including branded products in their videos. By incorporating products in a natural and authentic way, creators can earn money and provide their audience with a more engaging and authentic viewing experience. However, creators need to ensure that they are transparent with their audience about any product placements and that the products they feature align with their values and beliefs.

(11)

Influencer marketing: You can work with brands as an influencer to promote their products to your audience.

Influencer marketing is a popular form of collaboration between creators and brands, where creators are paid to promote a product or service to their audience. As a creator, you can work with brands as an influencer to promote their products to your audience, creating sponsored content that aligns with your channel and your audience's interests.

Influencer marketing can be a highly effective way for brands to reach new audiences and increase their visibility, while creators can earn money and build relationships with brands. However, it's important to ensure that the collaboration feels authentic and valuable to both the creator and their audience.

To be successful in influencer marketing, creators need to ensure that the products they promote align with their values and interests and are relevant to their audience. Creators can work with brands in a variety of ways, such as sponsored content on their channel or social media accounts, product reviews, or giveaways.

When working with brands, it's important to negotiate clear terms and expectations, such as the number of posts or videos required, the compensation, and any deadlines. Creators should also disclose any sponsored content to their audience to avoid misleading them, as required by the FTC.

To find brand collaborations, creators can reach out to brands directly, work with influencer marketing agencies, or join influencer networks. Influencer networks are platforms that connect creators with brands and streamline the collaboration process, handling negotiations, contracts, and payments.

It's important for creators to be selective about the brands they work with and ensure that the collaboration feels authentic and valuable to their audience. Creators should also maintain their creative independence and avoid promoting products that don't align with their values or interests.

In summary, influencer marketing is a popular way for creators to monetize their content on YouTube by working with brands to promote their products to their audience. By selecting the right brands and creating authentic sponsored content, creators can earn money and build relationships with brands while providing value to their audience. However, creators need to ensure that their collaborations feel authentic and transparent and that they maintain their creative independence.

(12)

YouTube Premium revenue: If your videos are part of YouTube Premium, you can earn a share of the revenue generated by the subscription service.

YouTube Premium is a subscription service that allows viewers to watch ad-free videos, download content, and access exclusive features such as YouTube Originals. As a creator, if your videos are part of YouTube Premium, you can earn a share of the revenue generated by the subscription service.

YouTube Premium revenue is distributed based on watch time, meaning creators who generate more watch time from Premium viewers will earn more revenue. The exact amount of revenue you can earn from YouTube Premium depends on various factors such as your audience, the type of content you create, and your geographic location.

To be eligible for YouTube Premium revenue, your videos need to meet certain criteria such as being advertiser-friendly and meeting YouTube's content policies. You also need to have at least 1,000 subscribers and 4,000 hours of watch time in the past 12 months to be eligible for the YouTube Partner Program, which allows you to monetize your content.

If you meet the eligibility criteria, you can opt-in to YouTube Premium revenue by going to your YouTube Studio and selecting "Monetization" from the left-hand menu. From there, you can select the option to enable your videos for YouTube Premium and agree to the terms and conditions.

It's important to note that while YouTube Premium revenue can be a source of income for creators, it's not a guaranteed revenue stream. The amount of revenue you earn can fluctuate based on factors such as viewer engagement and subscription numbers.

In summary, YouTube Premium revenue can be a way for creators to earn money on their videos if they meet the eligibility criteria and opt-in to the program. However, it's important to note that it's not a guaranteed revenue stream and can fluctuate based on various factors.

(13)

Content licensing: You can license your content to other websites, TV networks, or media companies, earning royalties for the use of your content.

As a YouTube creator, you can license your content to other websites, TV networks, or media companies, earning royalties for the use of your content. Licensing your content can be a way to expand your audience, gain exposure, and generate additional income.

To license your content, you can reach out to websites, TV networks, or media companies that you believe would be interested in using your content. You can also use licensing platforms such as Jukin Media, which can help you monetize your content by licensing it to brands and media companies.

When licensing your content, it's important to negotiate the terms of the agreement carefully. You should consider factors such as the duration of the license, the territories in which your content can be used, and the fees and royalties you will receive.

One advantage of licensing your content is that you can earn royalties for the use of your content without having to create new content. This means that you can earn money even if you take a break from creating content or if your channel experiences a downturn in viewership.

However, it's important to note that licensing your content may require you to give up some control over how your content is used. For example, the licensee may have the right to edit or modify your content, which could affect how your content is perceived by your audience.

In addition, licensing your content may require you to have ownership or control over the copyright to your content. If you use music or other copyrighted material in your videos without permission, you may not be able to license your content.

In summary, licensing your content can be a way to generate additional income as a YouTube creator. However, it's important to negotiate the terms of the agreement carefully and to ensure that you have ownership or control over the copyright to your content.

(14)

Product reviews: You can earn money by reviewing products related to your channel niche.

Product reviews are a popular way for YouTubers to earn money. Many brands and companies will pay creators to review their products, which can be an effective way to promote their products to a targeted audience. Here are some tips for earning money through product reviews on YouTube:

Choose products related to your channel niche: To ensure that your product reviews are relevant to your audience, choose products that are related to your channel niche. For example, if you have a beauty channel, you might review skincare products or makeup.

Be honest: Honesty is key when it comes to product reviews. If you don't like a product or don't think it's worth recommending, be honest about it. Your viewers will appreciate your honesty and are more likely to trust your reviews in the future.

Disclose sponsored content: If you are being paid to review a product, it's important to disclose this information to your viewers. This helps to maintain transparency and trust with your audience.

Show the product in action: When reviewing a product, it's helpful to show the product in action so that your viewers can see how it works. This can be especially useful for products that have unique features or functions.

Include affiliate links: To earn additional income from your product reviews, you can include affiliate links in the video description. This allows you to earn a commission when viewers click on the link and make a purchase.

Provide value to your viewers: Ultimately, the goal of your product reviews should be to provide value to your viewers. This means being informative, entertaining, and engaging. If your viewers find your reviews helpful, they are more likely to trust your recommendations and purchase the products you review.

In summary, product reviews can be a lucrative way for YouTubers to earn money. By choosing products related to your channel niche, being honest, disclosing sponsored content, showing the product in action, including affiliate links, and providing value to your viewers, you can create effective and profitable product reviews.

(15)

Public speaking: If you have a large following, you may be invited to speak at events or conferences, earning a speaking fee.

Public speaking is another way YouTubers can earn money. If you have a large following and are considered an expert in your niche, you may be invited to speak at events or conferences, either in-person or virtually. Here are some tips for earning money through public speaking:

Build your personal brand: To be considered a thought leader in your niche, it's important to build a strong personal brand. This means creating content that showcases your expertise, engaging with your audience, and developing a reputation for delivering quality content.

Network with event organizers: To get invited to speak at events, you need to be visible to event organizers. Attend industry events and conferences, and connect with event organizers on social media. Make it clear that you are available to speak at events and conferences.

Develop your speaking skills: To be an effective public speaker, you need to develop your speaking skills.

This means practicing your delivery, developing engaging content, and learning how to connect with your audience.

Set your speaking fee: When you are invited to speak at an event, you will typically be offered a speaking fee. Research the speaking fees in your industry, and set your fee accordingly. Be prepared to negotiate with event organizers to ensure that you are fairly compensated for your time and expertise.

Provide value to your audience: The key to a successful speaking engagement is to provide value to your audience. This means delivering content that is informative, engaging, and actionable. Make sure that your presentation is tailored to the needs and interests of the audience, and that you provide practical takeaways that they can apply to their own work.

In summary, public speaking can be a lucrative way for YouTubers to earn money. By building your personal brand, networking with event organizers, developing your speaking skills, setting your speaking fee, and providing value to your audience, you can establish yourself as a sought-after speaker and earn a significant income from speaking engagements.

(16)

Consultancy services: You can offer consultancy services related to your channel niche, such as social media marketing or branding.

Consultancy services are another way YouTubers can earn money. If you have a deep understanding of your niche and have built a following as an expert, you can offer your expertise as a consultant. Here are some tips for offering consultancy services:

Determine your niche: Identify your area of expertise and determine the services you can offer. For example, if your channel is focused on social media marketing, you can offer consultancy services on social media strategy, content creation, and audience engagement.

Define your services: Decide on the specific consultancy services you will offer, and outline the scope of each service. This will help you to set clear expectations with clients and ensure that you are able to deliver high-quality work.

Establish your rates: Research the rates charged by other consultants in your niche, and set your rates accordingly. Be prepared to negotiate with clients, but make sure that your rates reflect your expertise and the value you bring to the client.

Develop a portfolio: To attract clients, you need to demonstrate your expertise and the quality of your work. Develop a portfolio of case studies and client testimonials that showcase your consultancy services.

Network with potential clients: Reach out to potential clients through social media, email, or in-person events. Offer free consultations or workshops to demonstrate your expertise and build relationships with potential clients.

Deliver high-quality work: To establish yourself as a successful consultant, it's important to deliver high-quality work that meets or exceeds client expectations. Make sure that you communicate clearly with clients, set realistic expectations, and provide regular updates on your progress.

In summary, consultancy services can be a profitable way for YouTubers to earn money. By identifying your niche, defining your services, establishing your rates, developing a portfolio, networking with potential clients, and delivering high-quality work, you can build a successful consultancy business and earn a significant income from your expertise.

(17)

Book deals: If you have established yourself as an expert in your niche, you may be able to secure a book deal to share your knowledge.

As a YouTuber, if you have established yourself as an expert in your niche, you may have the opportunity to secure a book deal. Writing a book can be a great way to reach a wider audience and share your knowledge and expertise in more depth. Here are some tips for securing a book deal:

Develop a strong platform: Publishers are more likely to take a chance on a book by an author who has an established platform, such as a large following on social media or a popular YouTube channel. Build a strong online presence and engage with your audience to demonstrate your reach and influence.

Identify your niche: Determine your niche and the topics you are most passionate and knowledgeable about. This will help you to identify the target audience for your book and craft a compelling pitch.

Research publishers: Research publishers that specialize in your niche and have a track record of publishing successful books in your area of expertise. Make a list of publishers that align with your goals and submit a query letter or book proposal.

Craft a strong pitch: Your pitch should include a summary of your book idea, a brief bio that highlights your expertise and platform, and an outline of your target audience and the competitive landscape. Make sure your pitch is well-written and compelling.

Write a book proposal: Your book proposal should include an overview of your book idea, a chapter-by-chapter outline, and a sample chapter. It should also include information on your target audience, the competitive landscape, and your marketing and promotion plan.

Negotiate the contract: If a publisher is interested in your book, they will offer a contract. Review the contract carefully and negotiate the terms, including advances, royalties, and rights.

Writing a book can be a challenging and rewarding process, and it can also be a lucrative source of income for YouTubers. By building a strong platform, identifying your niche, researching publishers, crafting a strong pitch, writing a compelling book proposal, and negotiating a strong contract, you can secure a book deal and reach a wider audience with your expertise.

(18)

Brand partnerships: You can partner with brands on long-term campaigns or collaborations, earning a steady income over time.

Brand partnerships are a popular way for YouTubers to earn a steady income over time. When you partner with a brand, you typically create a series of videos that feature the brand's products or services. This can be a great way to generate buzz for the brand while earning money for yourself.

One benefit of brand partnerships is that they can be more lucrative than one-off sponsored videos or product placements. When you partner with a brand, you usually sign a contract that outlines the scope of the partnership and the compensation you'll receive. This can provide you with a reliable source of income over a longer period of time.

Another benefit of brand partnerships is that they can lead to other opportunities. For example, if you partner with a brand and create successful campaigns for them, other brands may take notice and reach out to you for similar partnerships. This can lead to even more income and exposure for your channel.

To secure brand partnerships, you'll need to have a significant following and engagement on your channel. Brands are often looking for influencers who have a large, engaged audience that aligns with their target market. You'll also need to have a clear understanding of your channel niche and the type of content that resonates with your audience.

When approaching brands for partnerships, it's important to be professional and to clearly outline the value that you can provide. This can include metrics such as your reach, engagement rate, and demographic information about your audience. You should also be prepared to provide examples of successful brand collaborations that you've done in the past.

In summary, brand partnerships can be a lucrative way for YouTubers to earn a steady income over time. By partnering with a brand, you can create successful campaigns that generate buzz for the brand while also earning money for yourself. To secure brand partnerships, you'll need to have a significant following, a clear understanding of your channel niche, and the ability to provide value to the brand.

(19)

Live events: You can organize live events, such as meet-and-greets or concerts, to connect with your fans and generate revenue.

Organizing live events can be a great way to connect with your audience and earn revenue outside of YouTube. Depending on your niche and the size of your audience, there are different types of live events you can organize.

For music creators, concerts are a popular option. You can perform your original music and covers, and even sell merchandise like t-shirts, posters, and CDs. You can also partner with venues or other artists to organize bigger events and reach a wider audience.

For vloggers and lifestyle creators, meet-and-greets are a great way to connect with your fans. You can organize these events at a public location, like a park or a mall, or partner with a business to host the event. You can sell tickets or charge for merchandise like autographed photos, t-shirts, or other branded products.

For educational or instructional creators, workshops or seminars can be a great way to engage with your audience in person. You can share your expertise in a specific topic and provide hands-on experience for your attendees. You can sell tickets to the event or charge for merchandise like books, workbooks, or other educational materials.

For gamers, organizing gaming tournaments or events can be a fun way to connect with your community. You can partner with other gamers or gaming companies to organize the event and provide prizes for the winners. You can also sell merchandise like gaming gear or branded t-shirts.

To successfully organize live events, it's important to plan ahead and consider logistics like venue, equipment, and staffing. You can also partner with other creators or businesses to help with the planning and promotion of the event. Social media platforms like Twitter, Facebook, and Instagram can be great tools to promote your event and keep your audience informed.

In conclusion, organizing live events can be a great way to connect with your fans and generate revenue outside of YouTube. Depending on your niche and audience size, there are different types of events you can organize, such as concerts, meet-and-greets, workshops, or gaming tournaments. It's important to plan ahead and consider logistics, and to use social media platforms to promote the event and engage with your audience.

(20)

Licensing music: If you create your own music for your videos, you can license it to other creators or media companies, earning royalties for its use.

If you create your own music for your videos, you can monetize it by licensing it to other creators or media companies. This can be a lucrative revenue stream, especially if your music becomes popular and widely used.

There are several ways to license your music, such as using a music licensing agency or selling licenses directly through your website. You can also offer different types of licenses, such as non-exclusive or exclusive licenses, depending on the needs of the licensee.

When licensing your music, it's important to set clear terms and conditions for its use, such as the length of the license, the territories where it can be used, and the media types where it can be used. You should also negotiate a fair price for the license based on the type of usage and the potential exposure of your music.

Overall, licensing your music can be a great way to earn money as a content creator, especially if you have a talent for creating catchy and memorable tunes.

www.ingramcontent.com/pod-product-compliance
Lightning Source LLC
Chambersburg PA
CBHW071028220526
45467CB00004B/1574

* 9 7 9 8 3 9 2 5 1 2 2 5 6 *